My First Pocket Guide

UTAH

By Carole Marsh

Correlates with Utah's CCSS Core Curriculum for Social Studies

THE UTAH ExperiencE

The GALLOPADE GANG

Carole Marsh
Bob Longmeyer
Chad Beard
Cecil Anderson
Steven Saint-Laurent
Jill Sanders
Kathy Zimmer
Terry Briggs
Pat Newman
Billie Walburn
Jackie Clayton
Pam Dufresne
Cranston Davenport
Lisa Stanley
Antoinette Miller
Victoria DeJoy
Al Fortunatti
Shery Kearney

Published by GALLOPADE INTERNATIONAL

www.utahexperience.com
800-536-2GET • www.gallopade.com

Gallopade is proud to be a member of these educational organizations and associations:

NSSEA

ASCD

SHOPA MEMBER
School, Home, & Office Products Association

Other Utah Experience Products

- The Utah Experience!
- The BIG Utah Reproducible Activity Book
- The Utah Coloring Book
- My First Book About Utah!
- Utah "Jography": A Fun Run Through Our State
- Utah Jeopardy!: Answers and Questions About Our State
- The Utah Experience! Sticker Pack
- The Utah Experience! Poster/Map
- Discover Utah CD-ROM
- Utah "Geo" Bingo Game
- Utah "Histo" Bingo Game

Word From the Author... (okay, a few words)...

i!
Here's your own handy pocket guide
bout the great state of Utah! It really
vill fit in a pocket–I tested it. And it really
vill be useful when you want to know a
act you forgot, to bone up for a test, or
vhen your teacher says, "I wonder . . ."
nd you have the answer–instantly!
Vow, I'm impressed!

et smart, have fun!
Carole Marsh

Utah Basics

Utah Geography

Utah History

Utah People

Utah Places

Utah Nature

Utah Miscellany

Jtah Basics explores your state's symbols and their special meanings!

Jtah Geography digs up the what's where in your state!

Jtah History is like traveling through time to some of your state's great moments!

Jtah People introduces you to famous personalities and your next-door neighbors!

Jtah Places shows you where you might enjoy your next family vacation!

Jtah Nature - no preservatives here, just what Mother Nature gave to Utah!

All the real fun stuff that we just HAD to save for its own section!

Who Named You?

Utah's official state name is...

Utah

Word Definition

OFFICIAL: appointed, authorized, or approved by a government or organization

Statehood:

January 4, 1896
Utah was the 45th state to join the Union.

What's In A Name?

Utah was named for the Ute Native American tribe, who lived in the mountains. The name Ute means "people of the mountains." The territory was then called the Land of the Utes, or Utah.

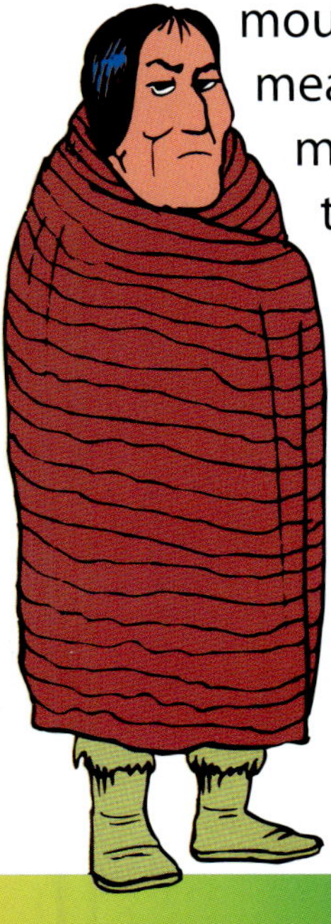

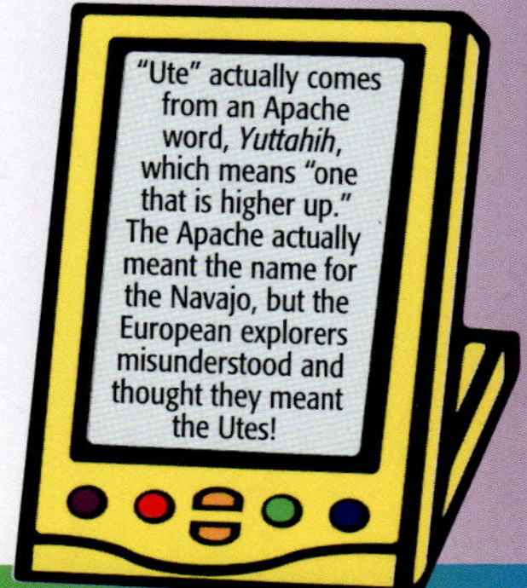

WHO Are You Calling Names?

Beehive State

Utah is not the only name by which our state is recognized. Like many other states, Utah has some nicknames, official or unofficial!

Mormon State

Salt Lake State

LAND OF THE SAINTS

State Capital:

Salt Lake City

Established 1847

Capital of Utah Since 1856

Salt Lake City was founded on July 24, 1847, by a group of 148 Mormons led by Brigham Young. By 1850, 5,000 Mormons lived in the community. The city was incorporated in 1851 and became the territorial capital of Utah five years later. The current capitol was completed in 1915, at the cost of $3 million! Its interior is decorated with marble. Four murals portray various historical figures, including Brigham Young and John C. Frémont.

The capitol's 284-foot (85-meter) high dome is covered with Utah copper.

Word Definition

CAPITAL: a town or city that is the official seat of government

CAPITOL: the building in which the government officials meet

State Government

Who's in Charge Here?

Utah's GOVERNMENT has three branches:

EXECUTIVE

A governor, lieutenant governor, attorney general, treasurer, and an auditor

LEGISLATIVE

Two Houses:
The Senate (29 members)
House of Representatives (75 members)

JUDICIAL

Supreme Court (five justices)
District Courts
Municipal Courts
Justice-of-the-Peace Courts
Circuit Courts
Juvenile Courts

The number of legislators is determined by population, which is counted every 10 years; the numbers above are certain to change as Utah grows and prospers!

State Flag

Utah's current state flag was adopted in 1913. It has a blue field (background). The state seal is in the center of the flag. The flag was designed in 1912 for the battleship *Utah*, which later sank in the 1941 Japanese attack on Pearl Harbor.

As you travel throughout Utah, count the times you see the Utah flag! Look for it on government vehicles, too!

State Seal

The state seal of Utah features a beehive, which stands for hard work and industry. There is also a bald eagle perched on top of the seal, which symbolizes protection in peace and in war. The sego lilies on either side of the beehive stand for peace. A U.S. flag appears on each side of the seal, which symbolizes Utah's support to the nation. The statehood year of 1896 is at the bottom of the seal.

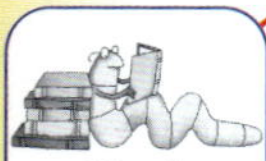

Word Definition

MOTTO: a sentence, phrase, or word expressing the spirit or purpose of an organization or group

State Motto

Utah's state motto is...

Industry

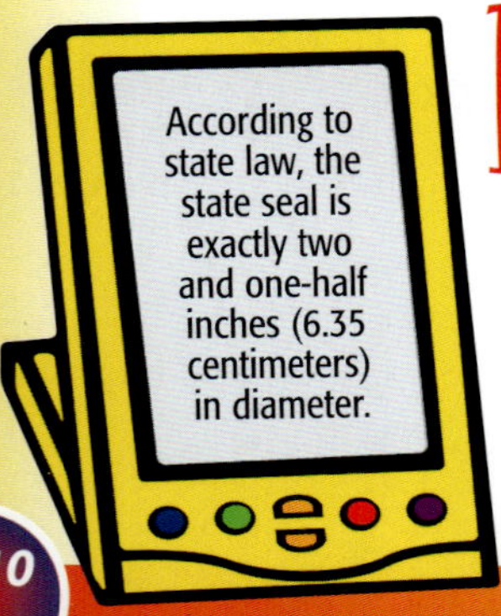

Birds of White Feathers

California Gull *(Larus californicus)*

It might seem strange for an inland state to have a "sea" gull as its state bird, but not all gulls live at the sea! When the Mormons settled Utah in 1847 and 1848, swarms of crickets appeared, devouring their crops. Luckily enough, flocks of California gulls swooped down and ate the insects! Utahns were so grateful that they made the California sea gull the official state bird on February 14, 1955.

Today, large colonies of gulls live along the Great Salt Lake and Utah Lake.

Blue Spruce

(Picea pungens Engelm)

Blue spruce can be found in the Wasatch and Uinta mountains at elevations between 6,000 and 11,000 feet (1,829 to 3,353 meters). Blue spruce have silver-blue needles. If you cut a spruce in half from top to bottom, both sides are symmetrical. Blue spruce grow well in cooler climates and are often used to make landscapes more attractive. The spruce also provides food for wildlife—some birds and hares eat the needles, deer eat the twigs, and small birds eat the winged seeds. Utah adopted the blue spruce as its state tree in 1933.

Sego Lily

A lovelier flower on earth was never sown.—William Wordsworth

The sego lily was adopted as Utah's state flower on March 18, 1911. The flower has white, lilac, or yellow blossoms. The sego lily grows to be 6–8 inches (15.2–20.3 centimeters) in height, during the summer months. When their crops were destroyed by the cricket swarms in the mid-1800s, the Mormons learned to dig up and eat the soft, bulbous root of the sego lily.

Early Spanish explorers called the sego lily the *mariposa*.

Riddle:

If the state flower got mixed up with the state bird, what would you have?

Answer:
A lily that can fly and eat crickets–if it could happen!

ROCKY MOUNTAIN ELK

State Animal

(*Cervus canadensis*)

The Rocky Mountain elk is a member of the deer family, and lives close to deer and moose throughout much of Utah. Mature bull (male) elks can stand up to 60 inches (152.4 centimeters) at the shoulder, and weigh more than 700 pounds (317.4 kilograms)! Utah officially adopted this majestic animal in 1971.

State Fossil

In 1988, Utah chose the *Allosaurus* to be its state fossil. The name *Allosaurus* has many different meanings, including "strange reptile" and "different lizard." *Allosaurus* was a carnivore (meat eater) that measured up to 16.5 feet (5 meters) in height and 39 feet (12 meters) in length. More than 60 *Allosaurus* skeletons have been found in various parts of Utah.

Coal

State Rock

The expansion of coal production has helped to make Utah's mining industry even more profitable. Coal comes from ancient plant matter that built up in wetlands and bogs long ago. Over millions of years, heat, pressure, and bacteria turned the plant material into a valuable energy source: coal! Emery and Carbon counties are where most of the Utah coal can be found.

The Cherry

After Millville Elementary second graders were asked what they thought the state fruit should be, they chose three possibilities: the peach, the apple, and the cherry. After many Utahns were polled, the cherry was adopted as the state fruit in 1997. Both sweet and tart (pie) cherries are grown in Utah. About 2 billion cherries are harvested every year, and about 4,800 acres (1,943 hectares) of agricultural land is devoted to cherry growing.

Topaz

Topaz became Utah's official state gem on February 4, 1969. Topaz can be found in many different colors, including orange, red, pink, beige, and green. Some are even colorless! Topaz has been used in jewelry for thousands of years, because it is both beautiful and durable. Topaz can be found in Beaver, Juab, and Tooele counties in Utah.

State Insect

Honeybee
– Apis mellifera

The honeybee became Utah's state insect in 1983. When the Mormons first settled in Utah, they called their new home the "Provisional State of Deseret." In the Book of Mormon, *Deseret* means "honeybee." Honeybees symbolize hard work and industry, so the insect matches up perfectly with the state's motto!

Utah's official state emblem is a beehive!

BONNEVILLE
Cutthroat Trout

—*Oncorhynchus clarki*—

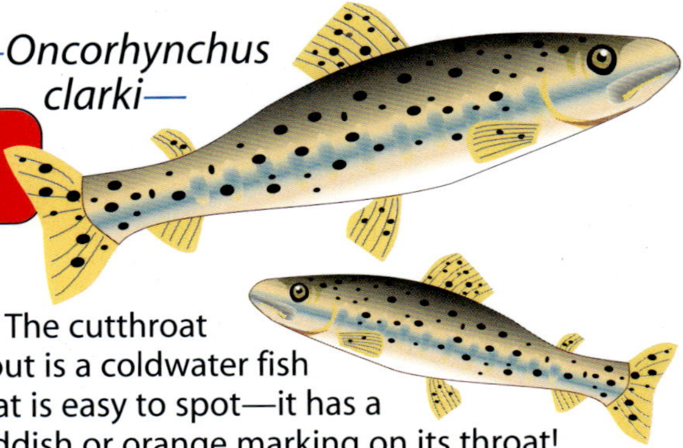

The cutthroat trout is a coldwater fish that is easy to spot—it has a reddish or orange marking on its throat! Utah's state fish is named for Lake Bonneville, which covered much of western Utah during the Ice Age. In fact, the Great Salt Lake is a remnant of that enormous prehistoric lake! The rainbow trout was Utah's state fish until 1997, when it adopted the Bonneville cutthroat trout to honor its importance as a food source for early settlers and Native Americans.

TASTY TROUT!

Put a trout filet on foil. Drizzle with lemon juice. Sprinkle with salt and pepper. Add shredded smoked ham and broil fish until done.

The State of Utah

About 25,000 years ago, an enormous body of water called Lake Bonneville covered western Utah. Over time, Lake Bonneville's waters dried up, leaving behind an immense land depression (low spot) called the Great Basin. Most of Lake Bonneville is gone now, but the Great Salt Lake and Lake Utah are souvenirs of this ancient watery area.

State Location

Utah is one of the Rocky Mountain states.

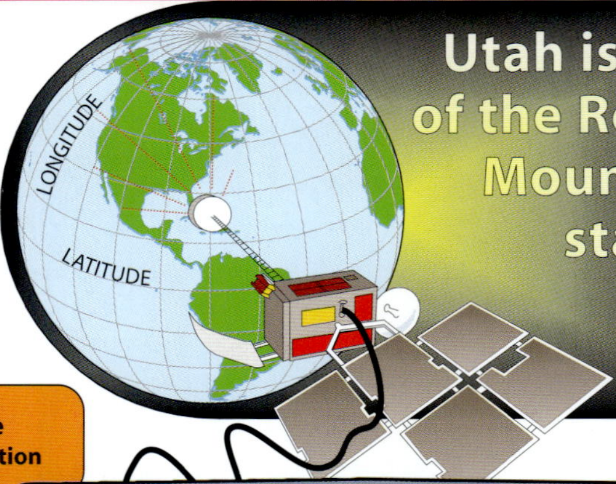

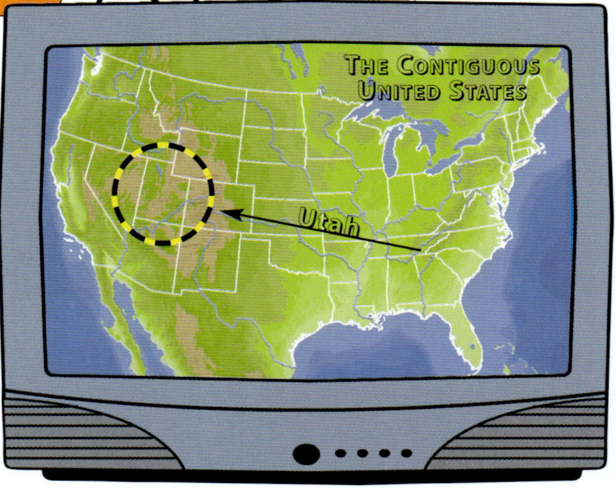

Word Definition

LATITUDE: Imaginary lines which run horizontally east and west around the globe
LONGITUDE: Imaginary lines which run vertically north and south around the globe

On The Border!

These border Utah:

States: Idaho, Nevada, Arizona, New Mexico, Colorado, Wyoming

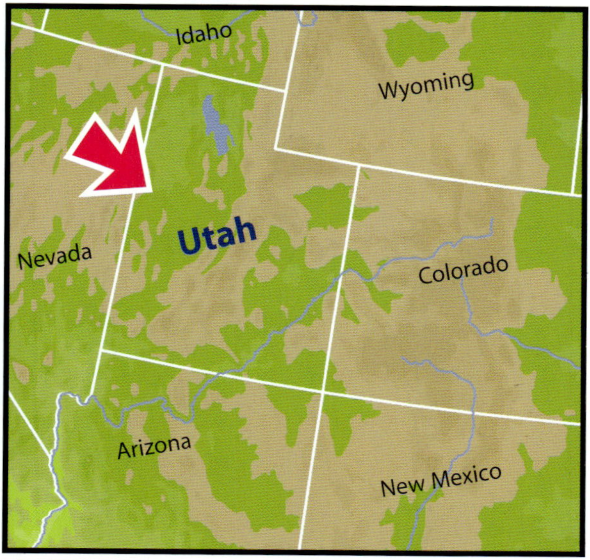

I'll Take the Low Road...

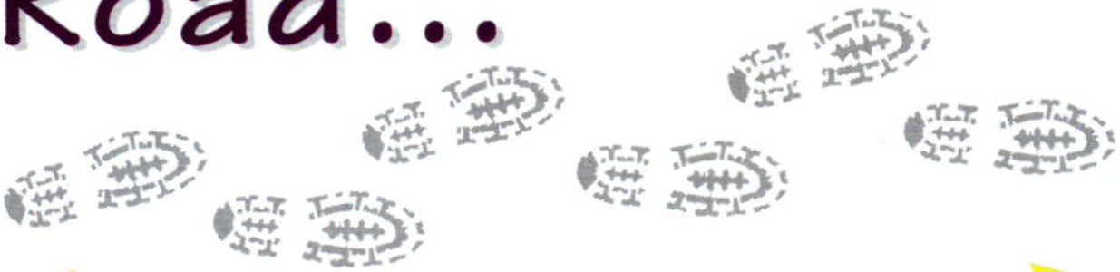

Utah stretches 345 miles (555 kilometers) from north to south—or south to north. Either way, it's a long drive!

Total Area: Approximately 84,904 square miles (219,884 square kilometers)
Land Area: Approximately 82,168 square miles (212,799 square kilometers)

Utah is 277 miles (446 kilometers) from east to west—or west to east. Either way, it's *still* a long drive!

You Take the High Road!

HIGHEST POINT

Kings Peak—13,528 feet (4,123 meters) above sea level

Kings Peak was named for Clarence King, an American geologist. King's mining surveys helped to open up the West for the Union Pacific Railroad. A plaque on the summit of Kings Peak commemorates King.

LOWEST POINT

Beaverdam Creek in Washington County—
2,000 feet (610 meters) above sea level

I'm County-ing on You!

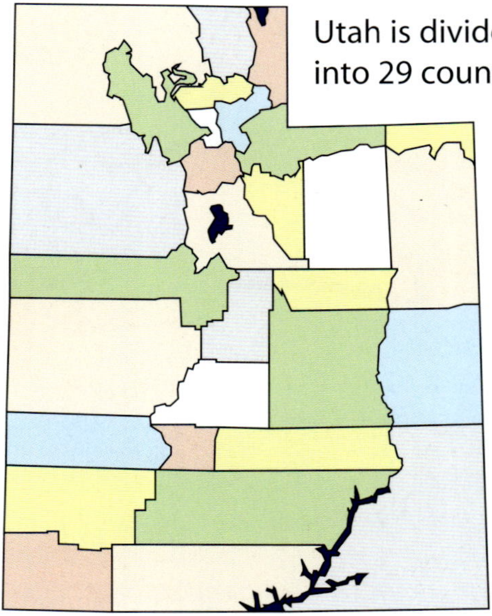

Utah is divided into 29 counties.

Word Definition

COUNTY: an administrative subdivision of a state or territory

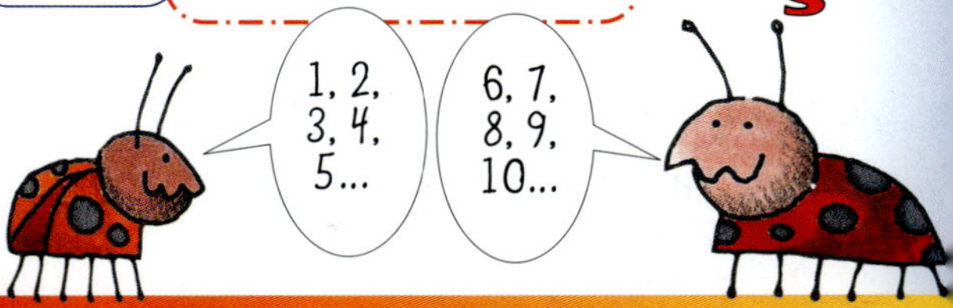

Natural Resources

It's All Natural!

Forests cover about 27 percent of Utah, but only about one-fifth of the forests are used for commercial forestry.

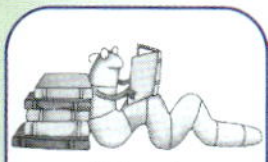

Word Definition

NATURAL RESOURCES: things that exist in or are formed by nature

Minerals and rocks:

- Iron Pyrite
- Quartz
- Calcite
- Pumice
- Mica
- Perlite
- Kaolinite
- Sandstone

Weather, Or Not?!

Utah's temperatures can drop to below 20°F (-7°C) in the winter and top 90°F (32°C) in the summer.

Highest temperature: 117°F (47°C), Saint George, July 5, 1895

°F=Degrees Fahrenheit °C=Degrees Celsius

Lowest temperature: -69°F (-56°C), Peters Sink, February 1, 1985

Utah's growing season lasts less than 90 days in the mountain valleys in the north to more than 200 days in other parts of the state.

Back On Top

Thousands of years ago, glaciers covered much of Utah, and have left their mark on the land. Utah is filled with snow-covered mountains, valleys, plateaus, and beautifully colored canyons. Wind and rain have worn Utah's rocks into many arches and natural bridges. Utah is also part of the Four Corners region, the only place in the United States where four states meet (the other three are New Mexico, Colorado, and Arizona).

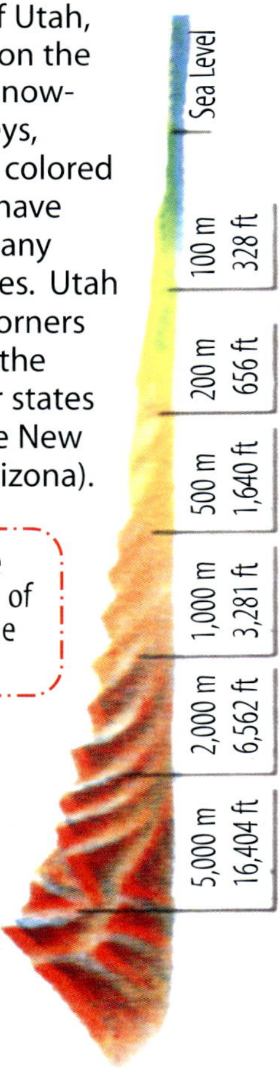

Word Definition

TOPOGRAPHY: the detailed mapping of the features on the surface of land

King of the Hill

Mountains

- Kings Peak
- Mount Timpanogos
- Mount Nebo
- Mount Belnap
- Mount Lovenia
- Mount Marvine
- Mount Peale
- Mount Pennell

Ranges

- Uinta Mountains
- Wasatch Mountains
- Confusion Range
- Hogup Mountains

A River Runs Through It!

Here are some of Utah's major rivers:

- Colorado River
- Green River
- Raft River
- Spanish Fork River
- Sevier River
- Ogden River
- Virgin River
- Bear River
- Provo River
- Jordan River
- Weber River

Gone Fishin'

Major lakes in Utah include:

- Great Salt Lake
- Utah Lake
- Lake Powell
- Bear Lake
- Flaming Gorge Reservoir

The Great Salt Lake is the largest salt lake in North America. The soil of the Great Basin gives the lake its high salt content. It is fed by three rivers (Bear, Weber, and Jordan) and has no outlet!

RESERVOIR: a body of water stored for public use

Cities & Towns

ARE YOU A CITY MOUSE... OR A COUNTRY MOUSE?

Have you heard of these wonderful Utah town, city, or crossroad names? Perhaps you can start your own list!

MAJOR CITIES:

- Salt Lake City
- Provo
- Orem
- Ogden
- Logan

UNIQUE NAMES:

- Dutch John
- Beaver
- Eden
- Elmo
- Eureka
- Gusher
- Helper
- Oasis
- Paradise
- Tropic

Transportation

Major Interstate Highways

There are about 41,341 miles (66,530 kilometers) of public highways in Utah, about 938 miles (1,510 kilometers) of which are national interstate highways.

I-80, I-15, I-70

Transportation

Railroads

On May 10, 1869, the first transcontinental railroad system in the United States was completed in Utah—the Central Pacific and Union Pacific railroads were joined at Promontory.

Today, there are about 1,420 miles (2,285 kilometers) of railroad track in Utah. The major railroad lines are the Union Pacific and the Burlington Northern Santa Fe. Ogden and Salt Lake City are important junctions on transcontinental railroad lines.

Major Airports

Utah has more than 80 airports, many of which are private. The major commercial airport is in Salt Lake City.

Timeline

1776 Friars Silvestre Vélez de Escalante and Francisco Atanasio Domínguez explore Utah
1825 Jim Bridger discovers the Great Salt Lake
1830 *The Book of Mormon* is published
1843 Captain John Frémont explores the Great Salt Lake region
1847 First Mormons arrive in Utah
1849 Brigham Young becomes governor of the Provisional State of Deseret
1850 Congress establishes the Utah Territory
1857 Utah War begins
1865 Ute-Black Hawk War begins
1869 Union Pacific and Central Pacific railroads meet in Promontory
1896 Utah becomes the 45th U.S. state
1915 State capitol in Salt Lake City is completed
1929 Utah's mining industry collapses after the stock-market crash
1942 Japanese Americans are interned in Millard County by order of President Roosevelt
1952 Uranium is discovered at Moab
1968 SOCIO (Spanish Speaking Organization for Community, Integrity, and Opportunity) is established
1982 Barney Clark receives the first artificial heart transplant at the University of Utah Medical Center
1991 U.S. government reimburses Utahns exposed to radiation in 1950s and 1960s experiments
2001 Utah enters the 21st century!

Here come the humans!

The first humans probably came to North America more than 14,000 years ago. Archaeological evidence suggests that some people came across a land bridge connecting Siberia and Alaska, and others sailed across the Atlantic Ocean from Europe.

The first people in Utah lived in natural caves and in the forests and mountains of ancient Utah. Many of their tools have been found, including chipped stone spear points and axes, and bone awls and scrapers.

Early Indians

Native Americans Once Ruled!

About AD 400, the Fremont people lived in Utah. They grew corn, squash, and beans, and lived in pit houses (shelters dug into the ground). The highly developed Anasazi culture also lived in Utah, and often built heir adobe pueblos on top of mesas. Both the Fremont and Anasazi people disappeared rom Utah by 1200. They may have left because of a long drought, or because other, nore aggressive groups were moving into the area.

Word Definition

ADOBE: brick made of clay baked in the sun, used in building

A New Land!

The first Europeans arrived in Utah around 1776. A group of Spanish missionaries led by friars (Catholic priests) came from Santa Fe, New Mexico. They were looking for an overland route to the Spanish missions in Monterey, California, and passed through Utah. Unfortunately, bad weather, short supplies and difficult terrain forced the missionaries to give up their expedition and return to Santa Fe.

Home, Sweet Home

After the first missionary expedition in 1776, Spain considered Utah part of its territory but didn't try to colonize it. In the early 1800s, Americans began coming to Utah from the East in search of furs. Mountain men explored the area, blazing trails and trading with the Native Americans.

In 1847, a group of Mormons arrived in the Salt Lake Valley. Brigham Young, their leader, declared that this place would be their new home. The Mormons built a fort from sun-dried adobe bricks, planted fields, and dug irrigation ditches. They named their new home Deseret, and many more Mormons came to the area over the next few years.

LIKE A NEW PENNY!

Copper is Utah's state mineral, and for good reason. Utah is the second biggest producer of copper in the United States! Copper is a versatile metal that is used in a variety of ways. Copper conducts (passes) heat and electricity well, is used in electronics and plumbing, and also is mixed with other metals in alloys.

Most of Utah's copper comes from the Bingham Canyon mine, southwest of Salt Lake City. The Bingham Canyon mine is the world's largest open-pit copper mine, and is 0.5 miles (0.8 kilometers) deep and 2.5 miles (4 kilometers) wide!

Why the North Star Stands Still—A Paiute Legend

Once, the People of the Sky roamed so much, they left trails in the heavens that we can watch now as stars. But, the North Star does not move. Long ago, the North Star roamed the earth and was called Na-gah. Na-gah liked to climb mountains, and one day found a mountain that seemed too high to climb. Na-gah found a tunnel that he followed all the way to the top of the mountain.

When Na-gah came out of the tunnel, he realized that he was much too high to climb back down. He was able to survive by eating grass until his father found him. Na-gah's father turned him into a star, so that Na-gah could live forever at the top of the mountain and never need to move. And that is why the North Star never moves!

Exploring Friars

Some settlers in the New World felt that England ignored their ideas and concerns. In 1775, the colonies went to war with England. On July 4, 1776, the Declaration of Independence was signed.

That same month, two Spanish priests named Silvestre Vélez de Escalante and Francisco Atanasio Domínguez set out from the New Mexico colony. They travelled westward, toward California. The friars entered Utah from the east and travelled along the White River to Utah Lake. They camped with a band of Ute there and promised to return later or send other missionaries. Unfortunately, that promise was never fulfilled; the next people to come to Utah were fur trappers in the 1800s.

Slaves and Slavery

In 1849, the Mormons established the Provisional State of Deseret, adopted a constitution, and asked Congress to be admitted to the Union. Unfortunately, Congress was in the middle of a bitter debate over slavery at that time. The main problem was whether the new territories the United States had gained in the Mexican-American War should be allowed to have slavery. Congress passed the Compromise of 1850, which created the New Mexico and Utah Territories. In both territories, the question of slavery was left up to the settlers to decide.

In 1852, the Utah state legislature legalized slavery. Some Mormons who came to Utah from southern states owned slaves, while other Mormon settlers did not. However, slavery ended officially in Utah in 1862 when Congress abolished slavery in the territories. In 1865, the 13th Amendment abolished slavery in the entire United States.

Word Definition

ABOLITIONIST: person who believed slavery was wrong and should be ended

Brother

The Civil War was fought between the American states. The argument was over states' rights to make their own decisions, including whether or not to own slaves. Some of the southern states began to secede (leave) the Union. They formed the Confederate States of America.

In 1861, the telegraph lines from the East and West met in Salt Lake City, creating the first transcontinental telegraph line. One of the first messages carried by that telegraph line was Brigham Young's message to President Abraham Lincoln, pledging Utah's support to the Union in the coming Civil War. Colonel Patrick Connor marched Union troops from California into Utah in 1862 to ensure the Utahns' loyalty and built Camp Douglas near Salt Lake City.

Word Definition

RECONSTRUCTION: the recovery and rebuilding period following the Civil War

vs. Brother

The Civil War was also called the War Between the States. Soldiers often found themselves fighting against former friends and neighbors, even brother against brother. Those who did survive often went home without an arm, leg, or both, since amputation was the "cure" for most battlefield wounds. More Americans were killed during the Civil War than during World Wars I and II together!

In 1863, the Emancipation Proclamation, given by U.S. President Abraham Lincoln, freed the slaves still under Confederate control. Some slaves became sharecroppers; others went to Northern states to work in factories.

Get It In Writing!

1776
Declaration of Independence

1789
U.S. Constitution

1830
The Book of Mormon

1849
Utah's first constitution
(as the State of Deseret)

1896
Utah's present constitution

WELCOME TO AMERICA!

People have come to Utah from other states and many other countries on almost every continent! As time goes by, Utah's population grows more diverse. This means that people of different races and from different cultures and ethnic backgrounds have moved to Utah.

In the past, many immigrants have come to Utah from Spain, England, Germany, Scandinavia, and other European countries. More recently, people have migrated to Utah from Hispanic countries such as Mexico, and from Asia and the Pacific Islands. Only a certain number of immigrants are allowed to move to America each year. Many of these immigrants eventually become U.S. citizens.

1848

A horrible swarm of crickets devours crops in Utah; sea gulls save the settlers by eating the crickets

1857

In the Mountain Meadows Massacre, a party of travelers passing through Utah are slaughtered

1900

An explosion in an underground mine in Scofield kills about 200 people

1927

An explosion at the Castle Gate coal mine kills 127 workers

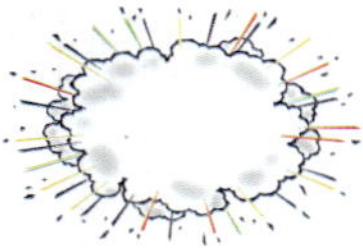

1968

In Tooele County, 6,400 sheep are killed by nerve gas that was being tested at nearby Dugway Proving Ground

1999

On August 11, a tornado rips through downtown Salt Lake City; over $100 million in damages

Legal Stuff

1850

Congress creates the Utah Territory

1862

Congress passes an antipolygamy law

1882

Congress passes the Edmunds Act, which takes the right to vote away from people who practice polygamy

1893

President Benjamin Harrison extends amnesty to polygamists

1895

Utah drafts a new constitution that outlaws polygamy and prevents the control of the state government by any church

Women & Children

1847

Utah's first school is founded at Salt Lake City

1850

Utah's territorial legislature provides for the creation of schools in Mormon settlements

1878

Utah's state legislature establishes a permanent, tax-supported school fund

1895

Utah drafts a new state constitution that outlaws polygamy

1896

Women gain suffrage; first two women are elected to Utah's state legislature

Fight! Fight! Fight!

Wars that impacted Utah include:

- Mexican-American War
- Utah War
- Ute-Black Hawk War
- Civil War
- Spanish-American War
- World War I
- World War II
- Korean War
- Vietnam War
- Persian Gulf War

Church of Jesus Christ of Latter-day Saints

The Church of Jesus Christ of Latter-day Saints was founded by Joseph Smith in 1830. Smith said that he had been visited 10 years earlier by the angel Moroni and given golden plates upon which a sacred message was inscribed. Smith translated the plates and published the message as *The Book of Mormon* in 1830. The church grew rapidly and had 1,000 members by the end of its first year. The Mormons moved into the Midwest and established communities in Kirtland, Ohio, and Independence, Missouri, during the early 1830s. The first Mormon temple was built in Kirtland in 1836.

About 20,000 Mormons then settled in Nauvoo, Illinois, in 1839. Unfortunately, Smith was killed in a riot in 1844; the church was then led by Brigham Young. In 1846, Young brought the Mormons westward, and they spent a harsh winter near Omaha, Nebraska. Finally, in 1847 the Mormons came to the Salt Lake area, where Young exclaimed, "This is the place!" The Mormons then made Utah their new home.

Indian Tribes

- Utes
- Shoshone
- Paiutes
- Gosiutes
- Navajo

The Ute were divided into eight different bands, including the Tampa and the Uinta. The bands didn't have a central government but shared the Ute languages and customs.

Nobody knows where the ancient Fremont people went. When the Ute and Shoshone people migrated into the Utah area, they may have made the Fremont people part of their own groups.

The Indians of Utah could not have known that the coming of the settlers would mean an end to the way of life they had known for hundreds of years.

Here, There, Everywhere!

SILVESTRE VÉLEZ DE ESCALANTE and FRANCISCO ATANASIO DOMÍNGUEZ were Spanish friars who first entered Utah from New Mexico in 1776. They were searching for a passage to California, without luck.

JIM BRIDGER was an explorer, trapper, and scout who discovered the Great Salt Lake in 1825. He also was the guide for Captain Benjamin Bonneville's 1832–1835 expedition into Utah.

JOHN CHARLES FRÉMONT was an explorer who surveyed much of the area between the Rocky Mountains and the Pacific Ocean.

PETER SKENE OGDEN was one of the first fur trappers to enter the Utah Salt Lake area.

JEDIDIAH STRONG SMITH came to the Salt Lake area around 1825 and was the first American to travel the length of Utah from north to south and from east to west.

Founding Fathers

BRIGHAM YOUNG—led the Mormons from Illinois to Utah; founded Salt Lake City and many other cities and towns

JOSEPH SMITH—founded the Church of Jesus Christ of Latter-day Saints (Mormons); was killed before his followers reached Utah

JOHN M. BERNHISEL—Utah's first territorial representative to Congress

HEBER WELLS—first state governor of Utah

Founding Mothers

EURITHE K. LABARTHE and SARAH E. ANDERSON—first women elected to the Utah House of Representatives

MARTHA HUGHES CANNON—defeated her husband to become Utah's first female state senator in 1896

SISTER MADELEVA—Catholic poet who founded the Saint Mary of the Wasatch women's college in the 1920s

REVA BECK BOSONE—elected Utah's first female judge in 1936

GREEN FLAKE, HARK LAY, and OSCAR CROSBY—African-American members of the first Mormon pioneer group to Utah (1847)

JAMES PIERSON (JIM) BECKWOURTH—explorer and mountain man; fur trapper with the Ashley company; published his memoirs, *The Life and Adventures of James P. Beckwourth* in 1856

JACOB DODSON—part of John C. Frémont's 1843 expedition into Utah

ALEX BANKHEAD—prominent Utah pioneer; remained in Salt Lake City when other African-Americans left after slavery was legalized in Utah; named his son Don Freeman Bankhead in honor of emancipation

ISAAC JAMES—he and his family were the first free African-Americans to settle in Utah; travelled with the Mormons from Illinois in 1847

LIEUTENANTS JOHN ALEXANDER and CHARLES YOUNG—two of only three African-Americans to graduate from West Point in the 19th century; served in the Ninth Cavalry (Buffalo Soldiers) at Fort Duchesne in the 1880s

BENJAMIN O. DAVIS, SR.—America's first African-American general; also served at Fort Duchesne briefly after the Spanish-American War

DID SOMEONE SAY BOO!?

The **Utah State Historical Society** in Salt Lake City is home to several ghostly inhabitants. A woman killed by a train while trying to get the ring her boyfriend threw on the tracks haunts the ladies' restroom and the cafe. People have also heard ghostly footsteps and voices and seen the apparition of an unknown man.

The **Hardy House Restaurant** in St. George is home to a strange shadow that has been seen by customers, wait staff, and the owner.

The ghosts of horses left to die of thirst long ago haunt **Dead Horse Point** in Canyonlands National Parks.

DO YOU BELIEVE IN GHOSTS?

TY DETMER—the first Utah college player to win college football's Heisman trophy (1990); played for Brigham Young University

ALF ENGEN—Father of Utah skiing; coached the U.S. Olympic Ski Team in 1948

JOHN STOCKTON—basketball point guard for the Utah Jazz; NBA record-holder for most career assists and most career steals

KARL "MAILMAN" MALONE—legendary basketball forward for the Utah Jazz

DANIEL AINGE—baseball and basketball player; played for the Toronto Blue Jays (baseball) and the Boston Celtics (basketball)

JAMES McMAHON—professional football player for the Chicago Bears

MERLIN JAY OLSEN—athlete, actor, and sports announcer; played college football for Brigham Young University; played professional football for the Los Angeles Rams

STEVEN YOUNG—played college football for Brigham Young University; professional football player for the San Francisco 49ers

GENE FULLMER—boxer; world middleweight boxing champion in 1957 and from 1959 to 1962

Entertainers

LORETTA YOUNG—actress; won the Academy Award for *The Farmer's Daughter* in 1947; hosted "Loretta Young Presents" on television (1953–1960)

DONNY and MARIE OSMOND—along with their five brothers, became internationally famous musical entertainers

HAL ASHBY—movie director and producer; best known for *Shampoo* (1975) and *Coming Home* (1978)

MAUDE ADAMS—actress; best known for performance as Peter Pan in a 1905–1907 run of *Peter Pan*

MAURICE ABRAVANEL—conductor and music director of the Utah Symphony from 1947 to 1980; built the Symphony into one of the nation's top orchestras

ROBERT REDFORD—actor, director, producer, founder of the Sundance Film Festival; won the 1980 Academy Award for directing *Ordinary People*

ROSEANNE—actress and comedienne

HAL ASHBY—actor; won the Academy Award for *In the Heat of the Night* in 1967

TONY GEARY—Emmy-winning actor

Authors

MAY SWENSON—poet, author, and teacher; won the 1981 Bollingen Prize in Poetry from Yale University

WALLACE STEGNER—won the 1972 Pulitzer Prize in fiction for *Angle of Repose*

ANN ELIZA YOUNG—one of Brigham Young's 27 wives; her 1878 autobiography *Wife No. 19* described life as a plural wife

KAREN SHEPHERD—journalist and teacher; founded, edited, and published *Network* magazine

MERLO JOHN PUSEY—won the 1952 Pulitzer Prize in biography and the 1952 Bancroft Medal for *Charles Evans Hughes*

HELEN ZEESE PAPANIKOLAS—historian and author; wrote several books focusing on non-Mormon Utah history

OTTO ABLES HARBACH—wrote the lyrics for around 50 musical comedies

BERNARD AUGUSTINE DE VOTO—Pulitzer Prize-winning editor, literary critic, and historian; wrote several books including *Mark Twain's America* and *The Course of Empire*

STEPHEN COVEY—author of *The Seven Habits of Highly Effective People*

FAWN M. BRODIE—author of *No Man Knows My History*, the first scholarly study of Joseph Smith

Riddle?

What famous American author wrote about his experiences in Salt Lake City in the book *Roughing It*?

Answer:
Mark Twain

Artists and Musicians

ALICE MERRILL HORNE—artist and state legislator who sponsored an 1899 bill to provide for annual art exhibits in Utah

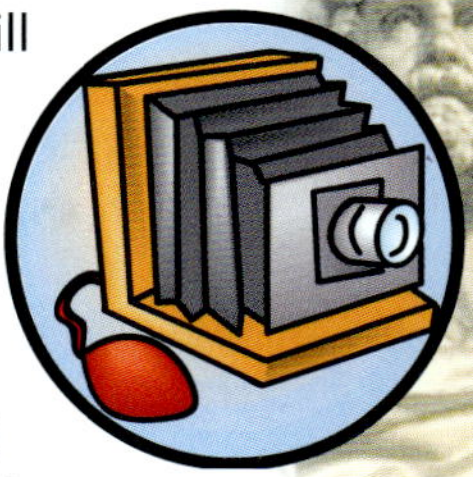

CYRUS E. DALLIN—sculptor best known for his Native American sculptures and a statue of the Angel Moroni on top of the Mormon Temple in Salt Lake City

MAHONRI YOUNG—sculptor commissioned by Utah to create a statue of his grandfather, Brigham Young; that sculpture was placed in the Capitol Rotunda in Washington, D.C.

TRUMAN O. ANGELL—architect who designed the Mormon Temple in Salt Lake City

EMMY LUCY GATES BOWEN—granddaughter of Brigham Young; Utah's first internationally famous opera star

GRANT JOHANNESEN—musician, first prizewinner of the Ostend International Competition in Belgium

Very Important People

MARRINER S. ECCLES—banker, economist, and government official; chaired the Board of Governors of the Federal Reserve System (1936–1948)

WILLIAM DUDLEY HAYWOOD—labor leader; led the Western Federation of Miners (1900–1905); helped found the International Workers of the World (IWW)

ESTHER R. LANDA—president of the National Council of Jewish Women (1975–1979); first director of University of Utah's Women Studies Program; cofounder of Project Headstart in Utah

JOHN WILLARD MARRIOTT—founded the Marriott Hotel and Restaurant chain

GEORGE WILCKEN ROMNEY—U.S. secretary of housing and urban development (HUD) from 1969 to 1972

TERRY TEMPEST WILLIAMS—led a crusade for a healthier environment; believed that chemicals and radiation from nuclear testing in Utah and Nevada caused illnesses in local residents

HELEN KURUMADA—civil-rights activist; first director of the Utah State Office of Asian Affairs

DANIEL JACKLING—founded the Utah Copper Mine Company

GEORGE SUTHERLAND—jurist; U.S. senator (1905–1922); associate justice of the U.S. Supreme Court (1922–1938)

WILFORD WOODRUFF—accompanied Brigham Young to Utah in 1847; his 1890 Woodruff Manifesto called for the end to polygamy

WILLEM KOLFF—developed the first useful artificial kidney

HARVEY FLETCHER—invented the hearing aid and the audiometer

PHILO TAYLOR FARNSWORTH—invented television

JOHN MOSES BROWNING—along with his brothers invented several types of rifles

ROBERT JARVIC—invented the first successful artificial heart

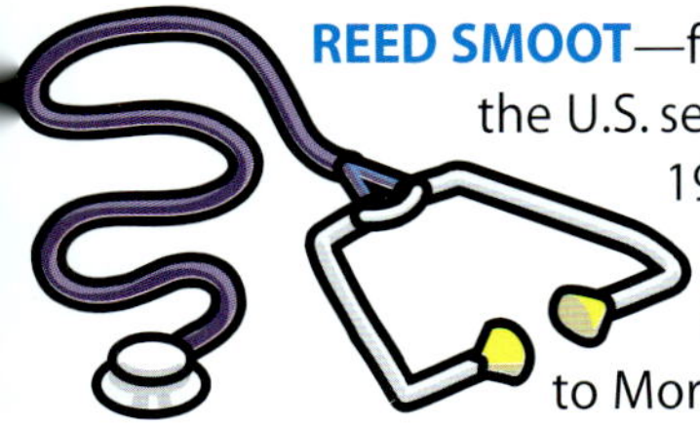

REED SMOOT—first Mormon elected to the U.S. senate; was elected in 1903, but unable to take his seat until 1907 because of opposition to Mormon practices

NOLAN KAY BUSHNELL—invented the first coin-operated video game

Political Leaders

- JEAN WESTWOOD—first female chairperson of the National Democratic Party
- OLENE WALKER—first female lieutenant governor of Utah (elected 1992)
- EZRA TAFT BENSON—U.S. secretary of agriculture (1953–1961); head of the Council of Twelve Apostles of the Church of Jesus Christ of Latter-day Saints (1973–1975)
- GEORGE H. DERN—governor of Utah (1925–1933); passed Utah's first income tax; U.S. secretary of war (1933–1936)
- EDWIN JACOB GARN—naval pilot and politician; mayor of Salt Lake City (1972–1974); U.S. senator (1974–1992); flew aboard the space shuttle *Discovery* in 1985
- ORRIN GRANT HATCH—U.S. senator (1977–); leading Republican
- DAVID M. KENNEDY—secretary of the treasury (1969–1971); ambassador to NATO (1971–1975)
- ESTHER E. PETERSON—assistant secretary of labor (1961–1969); special assistant to President Carter for consumer affairs (1977–1980); received the 1981 Presidential Medal of Freedom
- WALKARA—Ute chief; most powerful Native American leader in the Great Basin region from 1830 until 1855

GOOD GUY

BRIGHAM YOUNG—brought the Mormons from Nauvoo, Illinois, to Utah; founded Salt Lake City and helped found many other towns and settlements in Utah; had 27 wives and dozens of children; was the political and spiritual leader of the Utah settlers until his death in 1898

BAD DUDE

BUTCH CASSIDY—born George Leroy Parker; led a gang called "The Wild Bunch," including Harry Longabaugh (the Sundance Kid); hid out in Robbers Roost; went to live in South America when it became too hard to avoid capture in the U.S.; after robbing banks in several South American countries, was captured by Bolivian troops; nobody is entirely sure how he died

UNDECIDED

JOE HILL—a Swedish immigrant executed by firing squad in 1915 for the murder of a shopkeeper; evidence against him was circumstantial; many believe he was framed because of his involvement with coal-miners' unions in Utah

Keeping the Faith

Mormon Temple, Salt Lake City—ground was broken in 1853, and it took 40 years to complete; the center of the Mormon faith

Logan LDS Temple—third Mormon temple built in Utah; completed in 1884

St. John's Episcopal Church, Logan—built in 1909

Box Elder Tabernacle, Brigham City—completed in 1890, but destroyed by fire in 1896; renovations were completed in 1987

Mormon Tabernacle, Salt Lake City—built in 1867; home of the Mormon Tabernacle Choir

Provo LDS Tabernacle—completed in 1885

Saint Mary's of the Assumption Catholic Church, Park City—built in 1884

Schools

Utah State University, Logan—founded in 1888 as the Agricultural College of Utah

University of Utah, Salt Lake City—opened in 1850 as the University of Deseret; re-opened as University of Utah in 1892

Brigham Young University, Provo—began as Brigham Young Academy in 1875; now, is the largest church-sponsored university in the world

HISTORIC SITES

★ **Golden Spike National Historic Site**, Promontory Summit, west of Brigham City—honors the completion of the first transcontinental railroad in 1869

★ **Dinosaur National Monument**, north of Jensen—a quarry face where many dinosaur fossils were found and are still being excavated

PARKS

★ **Fremont Indian State Park**, southwest of Richfield—remains of an ancient Fremont village

★ **Bryce Canyon National Park**, Bryce Canyon—has been described as the most colorful national park in the world; displays limestone ranging in color from orange to white to red to purple

★ **Zion National Park**, near Rockville—Utah's oldest national park; has canyons and peaks with names like The Great White Throne, Angels Landing, and the Tabernacle

★ **Capitol Reef National Park**, near Fruita—is named after two unusual rock formations: the **Waterpocket Fold**, which resembles a coral reef on land, and the **Capitol Dome**, which looks like the dome on the U.S. Capitol in Washington, D.C.

Early Residency

★ Miles Goodyear Cabin, Ogden—built from cottonwood logs in 1846 by Utah's first settler; moved several times from its original location

★ Beehive House, Salt Lake City—Brigham Young's primary residence

★ John Platts Home, Salt Lake City—built by Brigham Young's carriage keeper in 1858

★ Reed Smoot Home, Provo—home of the Mormon apostle and first U.S. senator from Utah

★ Orson Hyde House, Spring City—the Mormon apostle's home from 1865 until his death in 1878

★ Jacob Hamblin House, Santa Clara—home of a Mormon missionary who was famous for his ability to keep peace with the Native Americans

★ Brigham Young Winter Home, Saint George—Young bought this house in 1870

★ Charles A. Steen House (Mivida), Moab—home of the man who discovered uranium near Moab

★ Arthur Taylor House, Moab—built in 1896

A few of Utah's famous Battles

- Comb Ridge, near Blanding—site of the last Indian war in the West, between the Ute and Paiute in 1923
- Mountain Meadows—site of the 1857 massacre of California-bound emigrants by Mormons and Native Americans; the Mormons believed the emigrants had been involved in the murder of Joseph Smith 13 years before

A few of Utah's famous Forts

- Fort Douglas, Salt Lake City—established in 1862 by Colonel Patrick E. Connor to both protect the telegraph line and to keep an eye on the Utahns
- Cove Fort, Cove Fort—built in 1867 to protect the Deseret Telegraph Line from attack
- Fort Cameron, Beaver—built in 1872 to house 250 federal troops sent to protect Utahns from Native American attacks
- Fort Duchesne, Duchesne—housed the Ninth Cavalry, also known as the Buffalo Soldiers, in the 1880s
- Fort Buenaventura, near Ogden—founded in the mid-1800s as a trading center and military outpost by mountain man Miles Goodyear

Libraries

Check out the following special Utah libraries! (Do you have a library card? Have you worn it out yet?!)

- HAROLD B. LEE LIBRARY, Provo—at Brigham Young University; holds nearly 2 million volumes

- MINERS HOSPITAL/PARK CITY LIBRARY, Park City—built in 1904 as Park City's first hospital; moved and converted into the town library in 1982

- MORMON FAMILY HISTORY LIBRARY, Salt Lake City—the largest genealogical library in the world

- LATTER-DAY SAINTS' CHURCH HISTORIAN'S LIBRARY, Salt Lake City—the best private library in the state; the largest collection of materials on Mormons and their faith

Zoos and Attractions

State Arboretum of Utah, Salt Lake City—more than 7,000 trees planted around the University of Utah's campus

Hogle Zoo, Salt Lake City—more than 1,000 animals, representing more than 300 species

Red Butte Garden and Arboretum, Salt Lake City—150 acres (60.7 hectares) of trees, shrubs, floral displays, and walking trails

Tracy Aviary, Salt Lake City—thousands of birds from around the world; many endangered species

Best Friends Animal Sanctuary, north of Kanab—home to more than 1,500 pigs, burros, rabbits, birds, cats, horses, and other companion animals; a safe haven for abused, neglected, and abandoned pets

Museums

- John B. Browning Firearms Museum, Ogden—displays firearms invented by Browning and his brothers
- Utah Field House of Natural History State Park, Vernal—an excellent collection of models, fossils, and dinosaur reconstructions
- Iron Mission State Park/Museum, Cedar City—displays more than 100 horse-drawn vehicles
- College of Eastern Utah Prehistoric Museum, Price—houses four complete dinosaur skeletons, including an *Allosaurus* named Al
- Utah Museum of Natural History, Salt Lake City—more than 200 exhibits; includes Utah wildlife, Jurassic period dinosaurs, and portrayals of ancient Indian life

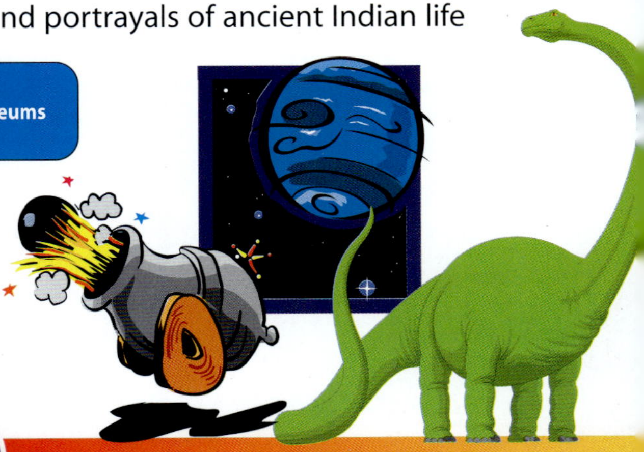

Lest We Forget

Mormon Battalion Monument, Salt Lake City—honors
ıe Mormons who enlisted to fight in the Mexican-
merican War

Seagull Monument, Salt Lake City—sculpted by Mahonri
ɔung in 1912–1913 to honor the gulls
ıat saved the harvest of 1848

Brigham Young Monument,
ılt Lake City—25-foot (7.6-meter)
'onze statue of the Mormon leader

This Is the Place Monument, Salt Lake City—marks the
estern end of the Mormon Pioneer Trail

Mormon Pioneer Memorial,
ılt Lake City—Brigham Young's burial site

Edge of the Cedars National Monument,
anding—a small Anasazi village that was occupied from
ɔout AD 750 to about AD 1220

Grand Staircase-Escalante National Monument,
calante—1.7 million acres (688,000 hectares) of incredible
ck formations, waterfalls, desert country, and more

Showtime

• Salt Lake Art Center—two-level gallery with locally significant art

• Utah Museum of Fine Arts, Salt Lake City—an extensive collection, including Egyptian, Italian Renaissance, and American art

• Sundance Institute, Provo—a combination of a resort, film workshop, artist colony, and environmental field laboratory founded by Robert Redford

• Utah Symphony, Salt Lake City

• Utah Civic Ballet, Salt Lake City—established in 1963

• Museum of Fine Arts, Provo—located at Brigham Young University

• Nora Eccles Harrison Museum of Art, Logan—20th century American art, Native American art, and fine ceramics

• Adams Shakespearean Theater, Cedar City—Elizabethan music and dance, spontaneous sword fights, and Punch and Judy shows, all found at Southern Utah University

Ruins

- Square Tower Ruins, part of Hovenweep National Monument, the Utah-Colorado line—Hovenweep is the site of six or more separate pueblo settlements that were abandoned around 1300; Square Tower Ruins is the best preserved of the pueblos
- Anasazi State Park, Boulder—an ancient pueblo; eighty-seven rooms have been uncovered, containing so many artifacts that a museum had to be built specifically to display them all
- Sand Island Campground, west of Bluff—large panels of ancient petroglyphs (rock carvings), including Kokopelli (a mythical Anasazi fluteplayer)

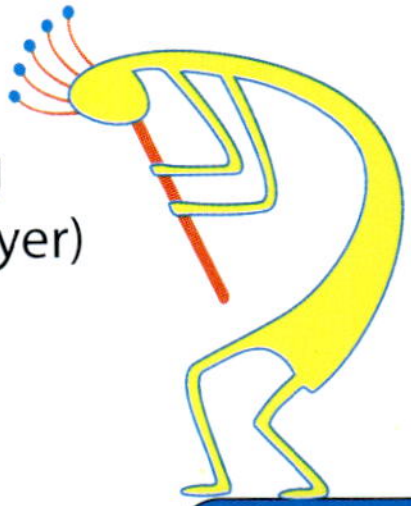

Reservations

- Ute Indians' Uintah and Ouray Reservation, northeastern Utah—the largest reservation completely within Utah's borders; has the Hill Creek Extension in eastern Utah
- Navajo Reservation, southeastern Utah—extends into Utah from New Mexico and Arizona
- Gosiute Reservation, near Gold Hill
- Kanosh Reservation, near Fillmore
- Koosharem Reservation, between Richfield and Robbers Roost

Logan Canyon—a 40-mile (64.4-kilometer) scenic route from Logan to Bear Lake; passes through the Wasatch-Cache National Forest

Ashley National Forest Scenic Byway—a 67-mile (108-kilometer) trip from Vernal to Manila; passes by Flaming Gorge National Recreational Area and several scenic outlooks

Mount Nebo Scenic Byway—a 38-mile (61.2-kilometer) route through the Uinta National Forest; several campgrounds, a natural rock amphitheater, the Mount Nebo Overlook, and much more

Colorado River Scenic Byway—44 miles (70.8 kilometers) from Moab; along the southeast side of the Colorado River; passes by Arches and Canyonlands National Parks

Trail of the Ancients—beginning at the Edge of Cedars State Park near Blanding; through many different Anasazi and other Indian ruins in the Four Corners area

LET IT SNOW!

Utah is home to 14 ski resorts, and Salt Lake City is the site of the 2002 Winter Olympics.

Alta, east of Salt Lake City—world-famous powder; quaint, laid-back resort; during World War II, the 10th Mountain paratroopers trained here

Snowbird, east of Salt Lake City—skiers ride trams to the top of the 11,000-foot (3,333-meter) high Hidden Peak

Brighton, east of Salt Lake City—named after William S. Brighton, who built a small hotel near the site of the present resort in 1874

Park City Resort, Park City—Utah's largest ski resort; can handle more than 20,000 skiers at once

Wolf Mountain, north of Park City—fifty-eight ski trails on three different mountains

Powder Mountain, northeast of Eden—has an incredible view

Nordic Valley, just west of Powder Mountain—all 12 runs are lit at night

Brian Head, east of Parowan—skiers take the lifts to the top of the 11,307-foot (3,426-meter) high Brian Head Peak

Utah's Animals Include:

- Elk
- Pronghorn
- Antelope
- Moose
- Bison
- Black Bear
- Cougar
- Rocky Mountain Goat
- Rocky Mountain Bighorn
- Coyote
- Bobcat
- Fox
- Badger
- Mink
- Otter
- Raccoon
- Weasel
- Skunk
- Porcupine
- Prairie Dog
- Rabbit
- Squirrel

The Gila monster, which is the only poisonous lizard in the United States, also lives in Utah!

Take a Walk on the Wild Side!

Some endangered and threatened Utah animals are:

Bonytail Chub
Humpback Chub
Kanab Ambersnail
Bald Eagle
Whooping Crane
Black-footed Ferret
Canada Lynx
Mexican Spotted Owl
Utah Prairie Dog
Desert Tortoise
Woundfin

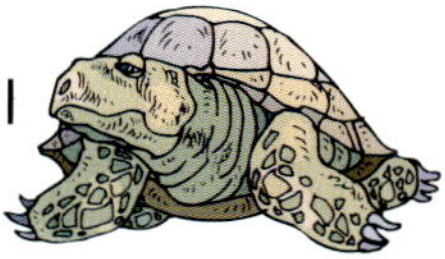

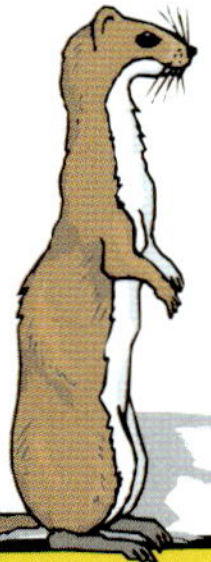

There are more than 20 endangered or threatened animals in Utah.

Birds

You may spy these birds in Utah:

Duck
Eagle
Grouse
Hawk
Heron
Magpie
Woodpecker
Owl
Pelican
Pheasant
Quail
Sea Gull
Titmouse
Goose
Warbler
Wren

Utah's endangered birds include the bald eagle and the whooping crane.

Don't let these Utah bugs bug you!

Mayfly
Damselfly
Cricket
Termite
Grasshopper
Giant Water Bug
Walking Stick
Spittlebug
Ant Lion
Ground Beetle
Whirligig Beetle
Sphinx Moth
Firefly
Ladybug
Stag Beetle
Weevil

Bumblebee

Ants

Butterfly

Praying Mantis

Honeybee

Ladybug

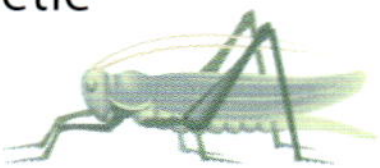
Grasshopper

Fish

Cutthroat Trout

Rainbow Trout

Brown Trout

Brook Trout

Largemouth Bass

White Bass

Perch

Whitefish

Carp

Catfish

Pond Critters

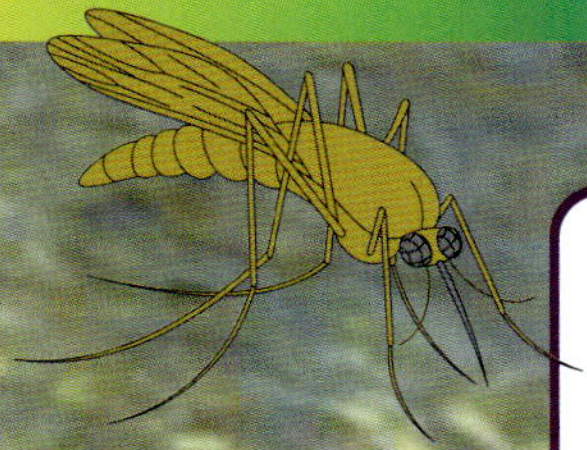

- Hydra
- Leech
- Freshwater Mussel
- Water Flea
- Freshwater Crayfish
- Fishing Spider
- Dragonfly
- Giant Water Bug
- Back Swimmer
- Water Strider
- Mosquito
- Minnow

Doctors once used leeches to cure illness. They thought the leech would suck out the disease!

Rocks & Minerals

Minerals are the building blocks of all rocks. A mineral can be as large as a person, but most are tiny and you will need a magnifying glass to see them clearly. Below are a few types of minerals that can be found in Utah.

- Olivine
- Hornblende
- Augite
- Feldspar

Rocks are solid masses of minerals or rock fragments that occur in nature. Below are a few types of rock that can be found in Utah.

- Meteorites
- Shale
- Mudstone
- Limestone
- Chert
- Flint
- Schist
- Slate

TREEMENDOUS!

These trees tower over Utah:

- Aspen
- Black Walnut
- Birch
- Balsam
- Blue Spruce
- Cottonwood
- Elm
- Fir
- Juniper
- Maple
- Oak
- Pine
- Sycamore
- Willow

Are you crazy about these Utah flowers?

- Sego Lily
- Chicory
- Goldenrod
- Fireweed
- Oxeye Daisy
- Prickly Pear
- Lupine
- Violet
- Wild Geranium
- Black-eyed Susan
- Indian Paintbrush
- Buttercup
- Queen Anne's Lace

Cream of the Crops

Agricultural products from Utah:

Poultry & Eggs

Hay

Peaches

Cherries

Pears

Beef Cattle

Sheep

Apples

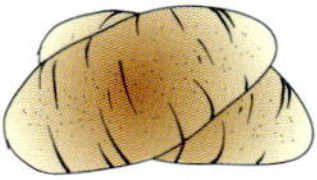
Potatoes

Dairy

Mink

Onions

First/Big/Small/Etc.

Levan is a town whose name is Navel spelled backwards—it's in the MIDDLE OF THE STATE!

There are at least 12 CANYONS in Utah named Long Canyon.

In 1992, Jan Graham became the FIRST FEMALE ATTORNEY GENERAL elected in Utah.

Reverend Robert Davis was the FIRST AFRICAN-AMERICAN ELECTED TO THE UTAH LEGISLATURE in 1976.

Utah's FIRST SALES TAX was introduced in 1933.

Utah's FIRST STREETCAR LINE was established in Salt Lake City in 1872.

The FIRST TRANSCONTINENTAL TELEPHONE LINE was completed in 1914 at Wendover, on the Utah-Nevada border.

The battleship USS *Utah* sank at PEARL HARBOR on December 7, 1941, when Japanese bomber planes attacked.

RAINBOW BRIDGE in southern Utah is the WORLD'S LARGEST NATURAL BRIDGE.

Celebrate!!!

Festival of the American West, Logan—begins the last Friday of July and continues for eight days; attendees pan for gold, visit a military camp, see a Wild West show in a saloon, and much more

Sundance Film Festival, Park City—a ten-day event every January founded by Robert Redford; an important showplace for independently produced films

Days of '47, Salt Lake City and **Pioneer Days**, Ogden—the week of July 24; celebrations of Utah's first settlement in 1847; rodeos, pageants, parades, and more

Arts Festival, Tooele—June; artists and craftspeople from around the West display their work

Western Stampede, West Jordan—early July; one of the West's liveliest rodeos

Utah State Fair, Salt Lake City—September

America's Opening, Park City—November; features ski racing and exhibitions

Holidays

Calendar

Martin Luther King, Jr. Day, *3rd Monday in January*

Presidents' Day, *3rd Monday in February*

Memorial Day, *last Monday in May*

Independence Day, *July 4*

Pioneer Day, *July 24*

Labor Day, *1st Monday in Septembe*

Columbus Day, *2nd Monday in October*

Veterans Day, *November 11*

Christmas Day, *December 25t*

PIONEER DAY CELEBRATES THE FIRST PERMANENT SETTLEMENT OF UTAH BY BRIGHAM YOUNG IN 1847.

Utah celebrates its admission to the U.S. on January 4.

Delicious Dishes

You can feast upon these yummy foods in Utah!

- Casseroles
- Broiled fish
- Chimichangas
- Chili
- Enchiladas
- Souvlaki
- Cinnamon buns
- Noodle salad
- Yeast bread
- Roast lamb
- Brisket
- Risotto
- Turnovers
- Kababs
- Cornbread
- Stroganoff
- Red beans and rice

Utah Works!

Utah has a diverse economy with several major industries including:

LIVESTOCK

Sales of beef cattle and dairy products are the biggest agricultural industries in Utah. Utahns also raise poultry, and Utah produces the most mink pelts in the United States.

MANUFACTURING

Most of the factories in Utah are located between Brigham City and Provo, especially around Salt Lake City. The most important manufacturing industry is the production of industrial machinery and equipment. Utahns also manufacture computers and office equipment, transportation equipment, chemicals, pharmaceuticals, and other things!

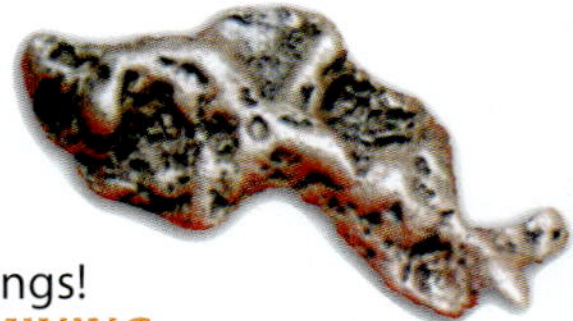

MINING

Utah is a leading copper-producing state, and both coal and petroleum production are important, too. Silver and gold were discovered in Bingham Canyon in 1863, and those metals are still mined there. Utah also produces natural gas, magnesium, cement, mercury, molybdenum, lime, and many other minerals.

Utah Books & Websites

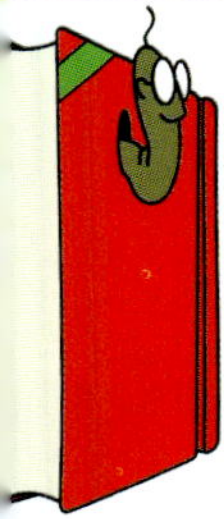

My First Book About Utah by Carole Marsh

America the Beautiful: Utah by Deborah Kent

Kids Learn America by Patricia Gordon and Reed C. Snow

Let's Discover the States: Utah by the Aylesworths

The Utah Experience Series by Carole Marsh

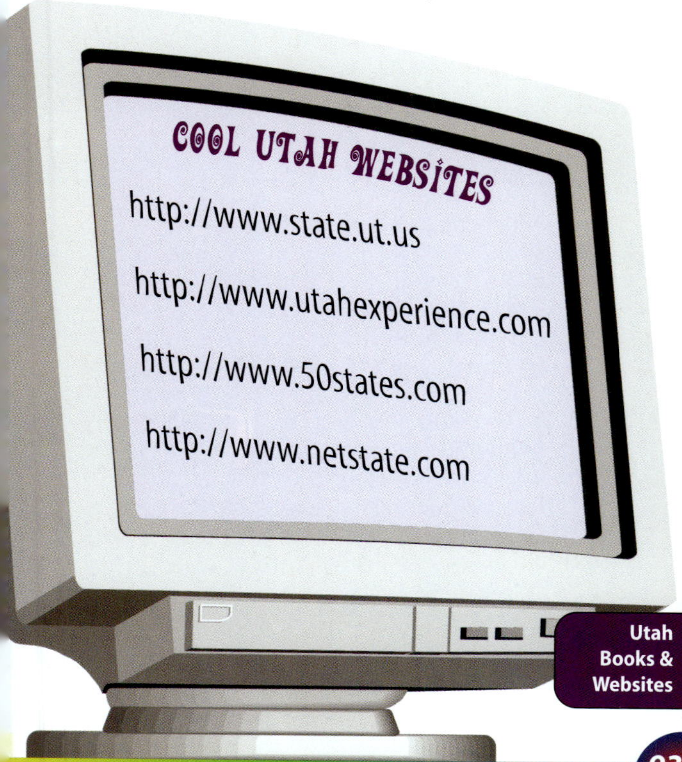

Utah Glossary

Glossary Words

commemorate: to honor the memory of

Deseret: a region in the western United States organized by the Mormons in 1849, part of which later became the state of Utah

glacier: a large mass of ice that moves slowly along the ground

industry: steady effort, hard work

interned: kept confined, often by an enemy, until the end of a war

polygamy: having more than one wife at a time

prehistoric: belonging to the time before history was written

provisional: temporary

symmetrical: the same on both sides, like a mirror image

tabernacle: a place of worship for a large congregation

Utah Spelling Bee

Here are some special Utah-related words to learn! To take the Spelling Bee, have someone call out the words and you spell them aloud or write them on a piece of paper.

Spelling Words

Allosaurus	Hovenweep
Anasazi	manufacturing
antelope	Navajo
Beckwourth	promontory
beehive	reservation
Bonneville	Sundance
Brigham	tabernacle
Deseret	Uinta
Escalante	university
government	Wasatch

ABOUT THE AUTHOR...

CAROLE MARSH has been writing about Utah for more than 20 years. She is the author of the popular *Utah State Stuff Series* for young readers and creator along with her son, Michael Marsh, of Utah *Facts and Factivities*, a CD-ROM widely used in Utah schools. The author of more than 100 Utah books and other supplementary educational materials on the state, Marsh is currently working on a new collection of Utah materials for young people. Marsh correlates her Utah materials to the Utah learning standards. Many of her books and other materials have been inspired by or requested by Utah teachers and librarians.

EDITORIAL ASSISTANT:

Antoinette R. Miller

GRAPHIC DESIGNER:

Cecil Anderson